B.C. I Don't Wanta Hear About It

Johnny Hart

CORONET BOOKS
Hodder and Stoughton

First published in the United States of America by Ballantine Books.

Coronet edition 1985.

British Library C.I.P.

Hart, Johnny
B.C., I dont wanta hear about it.—(Coronet books)
1. American wit and humor, Pictorial
I. Title
741.5′973 PN6737.H3

ISBN 0-340-37904-9

The characters and situations in this book are entirely imaginary and bear no relation to any real person or actual happening.

Printed and bound in Great Britain for Hodder and Stoughton Paperbacks, a division of Hodder and Stoughton Ltd., Mill Road, Dunton Green, Sevenoaks, Kent (Editorial Office: 47 Bedford Square, London, WC1 3DP) by Hunt Barnard Printing Ltd., Aylesbury, Bucks.

de·fect'

5·28

to rip off somebody's fect.

hart

SEE DICK CAMPAIGN
WITH JANE FOR
EQUAL RIGHTS.

5·30

SEE DICK GET
AN OFFICE JOB.

WHEN WATER DOTH DISGUISE ITSELF,
WITH NAMES AND STATES SO SUBTLE -
5·31

LIKE OCEAN, CREEK AND RIVER,
AND LIKE POOL OR POND OR PUDDLE -

OR SNOW OR RAIN OR HAIL OR FOG,
OR ICE OR CLOUDS OR GEYSER,

IT DOTH BEHOOVE AN "ANTI-WATER-FREAK,"
....TO BE THE WISER

LOOK, LOOK, SEE HIM GO TO THE MARKET.

HI. WHO ARE YOU READING ABOUT?

6·2

IT'S CALLED, "THE MYSTERY OF MISTER REEZE."

I'M IMPRESSED. WHO'S IT ABOUT?

SEE DICK TRADE IN
HIS GAS GUZZLER
ON A HORSE.

SEE DICK COLLECT
HIS REBATE.
6-3

SEE DICK BLOW HIS
REBATE ON AN OAT
GUZZLER.

MAY YOU TRY TO BREAK UP A FIST FIGHT BETWEEN A "MEAT AND POTATOES" MAN AND A "STOVE-TOP DRESSING" FREAK.
THE CURSE EXCHANGE
6·6

MAY A TALL GOAT EAT YOUR EAVES-TROUGH, DURING THE MONSOON SEASON.
THE CURSE EXCHANGE

THE CURSE EXCHANGE

MAY A CRICKET TAKE UP RESIDENCE IN YOUR DOCTOR'S STETHOSCOPE JUST BEFORE YOUR ANNUAL CHECK-UP.
THE CURSE EXCHANGE
6·7

MAY AN OVERZEALOUS SIDING SALESMAN SCOTCHTAPE 5000 WOODPECKERS TO YOUR HOUSE.
THE CURSE EXCHANGE

THE CURSE EXCHANGE

MAY A BURLY PERSON TAKE EXCEPTION TO THE WAY YOUR FACE IS ARRANGED.
THE CURSE EXCHANGE
68

MAY YOU BE HELD HOSTAGE FOR THE RELEASE OF THE UNKNOWN SOLDIER'S GRANDMOTHER.
THE CURSE EXCHANGE

THE CURSE EXCHANGE

MAY YOUR BLIND DATE INSIST ON WEARING A SKI-MASK.
THE CURSE EXCHANGE
6-9

MAY AN ABNORMAL PERSON TALK YOU INTO JOINING A RELIGIOUS SECT THAT EATS PING-PONG PADDLES.
THE CURSE EXCHANGE

THE CURSE EXCHANGE

MAY YOU FORGET YOUR BEST FRIEND'S NAME AS YOU DELIVER HIS EULOGY.
THE CURSE EXCHANGE
6·10

MAY AN INSINCERE GLASSBLOWER GIVE YOU MOUTH-TO-MOUTH RESUSCITATION.
THE CURSE EXCHANGE

THE CURSE EXCHANGE

MAY A SMALL RODENT FIND HIS WAY INTO YOUR JODHPURS.
THE CURSE EXCHANGE
6·11

MAY YOUR PRIEST OFFER TO SELL YOU A TAPE RECORDING OF YOUR LAST CONFESSION.
THE CURSE EXCHANGE

THE CURSE EXCHANGE

DEAR FAT BROAD,
MY MOTHER-IN-LAW IS ALWAYS LOOKING FOR DUST IN MY HOUSE...

6.21

DEAR FRUSTRATED,
WHY INVITE HER? JUST MAIL HER THE DUST.

DEAR FAT BROAD,
I DONT HAV AN EDJAKASHUN AN I FEEL DUM. WOT SHOOD I DO ?...
ADVICE COLUMN
625

P.S. MY HUZBIND IS RITEING THIS FOR ME.
FEALING DUM.

DEAR FEELING DUMB,
SEND YOUR HUSBAND TO SCHOOL.
ADVICE COLUMN

6·28

LOOKOUT!
THE LOOKOUT
6·29

WHAT....
THE LOOKOUT

ZAK!

TELEGRAM FROM YOUR
UNCLE FRIGGY.

6·30

RETURN IT.
HE PROBABLY JUST
WANTS MONEY.
WHERE'S
MY TIP?

YOU'RE WORKING WITH
UNCLE FRIGGY, RIGHT?

HEY, HAL, YOU FORGOT YOUR LUNCH!
7.2

I'LL GRAB A QUICKIE AT SHIRLEY'S TRUCK STOP.

DR. PETER ⟷ HEAD SHRINKER
I DREAMED I WAS A WARTHOG. DOES THAT MEAN I'M SICK?
DID YOU DO ANYTHING BAD?

7·5

I DON'T REMEMBER ...I WAS TOO BUSY WOLFING DOWN WARTS.

YOU'RE FINE! ...ME,....I THINK I'M GOING TO BE REAL SICK!

WHERE IN THE WORLD HAVE YOU BEEN ?

STOMPING GRAPES FOR WINE.
HOW COME YOUR ARMS ARE BLUE?

I HAD TO CLEAN OFF THE CUTE CHICK'S LEGS.

TARZAN GO! ...JANE STAY!
THUMP
THUMP

SUITS ME.
...SHOVE
OFF.
7·8

I'M GOING FISHING FOR LUNCH TODAY.

...I'M USING WORMS THAT HAVE BEEN MARINATING IN PEANUT OIL, FLOUR, RASPBERRIES AND YEAST FOR ABOUT THREE AND A HALF WEEKS.

WHAT DO YOU EXPECT TO CATCH WITH THAT?

A PEANUT BUTTER AND JELLY SANDWICH.

I'D LIKE A SCALE DRAWING OF A YANKEE CLIPPER WITH FULL SAILS PUT ON MY CHEST.
THOR'S TATTOO PARLOR

HOW ABOUT A NICE INNER TUBE WITH JOE DIMAGGIO'S INITIALS ON THE SIDE ?
THOR'S TATTOO PARLOR
1·11

?
7.13

THIS IS THE FCC, THE OCEAN'S ROAR YOU ARE ABOUT TO HEAR IS COMING TO YOU ON AN ASSIGNED FREQUENCY OF...

...SO THE HARE STOPPED OFF TO GRAZE IN A MARIJUANA PATCH AND GOT SO SPACED OUT THAT THE TORTOISE WON.
7.15

SOUNDS LIKE A FIX TO ME.

DRUNK AGAIN, EH?
YEP.

DID YOU PLAY CARDS AGAIN?
YES, AND I LOST A BUNDLE!
7·27

HOW CAN YOU STAND THERE AND GRIN THAT SILLY GRIN?

YOU'RE THE BUNDLE.....
hart

DO YOU HAVE ANY LOUIE THE 14TH SOFAS?
PETER'S CUT-RATE STORE
7-30

YOU'RE IN LUCK,...

WE HAVE THEM MARKED DOWN TO LOUIE THE 13TH.
PETER'S CUT-RATE STORE
hart

PICK

SHE LOVES ME,
SHE LOVES ME NOT...
PICK
PICK
PICK
PICK
8.3
SHE LOVES ME!

I HATE HER....

WHAT THRESHOLD OF PAIN DO I HAVE TO ENDURE TO HAVE A TATTOO?
THOR'S TATTOO PARLOR

FIFTY BUCKS AN HOUR.
THOR'S TATTOO PARLOR

8.5

FOR 200 BUCKS, I'LL SELL YOU THE ANTEATERS WHEREABOUTS EVERY DAY FOR A YEAR.

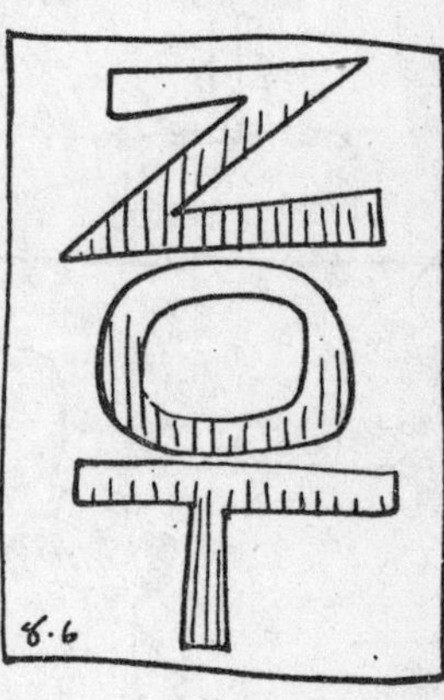
ZOT
8·6

THERE GOES THE LAST OF THE REAL "CLASS STOOLIES."

I FINALLY FIGURED OUT THE SECRET OF LIFE
8.9

NO KIDDING! WHAT IS IT ?

I AIN'T TELLING.

I UNDERSTAND YOU CAME FROM A SMALL TOWN.
THAT'S RIGHT.

HOW SMALL WAS IT?
8·11

THE SCHOOLBUS WAS A SKATEBOARD.
hart

HE WHEELS, FAKES, TUCKS, AND ANGLES THROUGH THE SLOT TO FIND THAT CHUNK OF REAL ESTATE FOR 7 POINTS
PLAY BY PLAY
COLOR

PLAY BY PLAY
COLOR

8·12

YOU'RE TRYING TO 'SLICK-TALK' US JOCKS OUT OF BUSINESS, AREN'T YOU!
PLAY BY PLAY
COLOR

WHATCHA DOIN'?
I'M EMBROIDERING A DECORATIVE BORDER AROUND MY APRON.

HEY, THAT'S A CUTE IDEA,... CAN YOU DO ONE ON MINE?
8·13

I CAN IF MY LIFE EXPECTANCY GOES UP.

WHAT'S UNDER THE SHEET?
8-15

MY GREATEST INVENTION.... THE MO-PED!
WHAT THE HECK IS A MO-PED?

A VEHICLE THAT LETS YOU PUMP INTO A GAS STATION.
hart

8-17

OK, THEN YOUR WIFE'S GOT SOMETHING GOING WITH 12 GUYS IN FUNNY HATS AND RUBBER BOOTS.

I'VE COME UP WITH A DEVICE THAT ELIMINATES HOUSEHOLD PESTS.
PETER'S PATENT OFFICE
8-18

WHAT'S THAT?

THE DIVORCE.
PETER'S PATENT OFFICE
hart

what the father of the bride says after blowing 500 bucks on her wedding gown.

I'D LIKE TO PATENT A CONGRESSMAN DOLL.
PETER'S PATENT OFFICE

8.20

DO YOU HAVE A WORKING MODEL?
PETER'S PATENT OFFICE

YOU GOTTA BE KIDDING!
PETER'S PATENT OFFICE

8·22

YOUR BIRTH CERTIFICATE.

ZANG

AFTER WE DOMINATE MAN, THINGS ARE GOING TO BE DIFFERENT!
8·23

IN WHAT WAY?

FOR ONE THING, THE CHOW IS GOING TO BE TERRIBLE.

DO YOU BELIEVE THERE IS A LIFE AFTER DEATH?

I HOPE NOT,...

8·24

...THE ONE BEFORE DEATH IS KILLING ME.

DO YOU FEEL THAT PEOPLE ON "FIXED" INCOMES SHOULD PAY TAXES?

8·26

DARN RIGHT! JUST BECAUSE A BOXER TAKES A DIVE IS NO EXCUSE FOR NOT PAYING HIS SHARE.

...I'LL JUST MARK THAT "NOBODY HOME."
HART

MY MOTTO IS:
"YOU GET OUT OF LIFE
WHAT YOU PUT INTO IT."

8·27

....I DON'T GET IT...

THERE YOU ARE.

gnat

WILEY'S
DICTIONARY

8-29

a gnickname for gnathaniel.
WILEY'S
DICTIONARY
hart

STOMP STOMP

PICK UP YOUR FEET, YOU BIG LUMMOX!
8·30

HE WOULDN'T TALK LIKE THAT IF HE KNEW I HAD A BLACK BELT.
hart

TENNIS ANYONE?
8·31

INTENSIVE CARE, ANYONE?

hart

HMM, INTERESTING...
THIS GLACIER HAS MOVED
A QUARTER OF AN INCH
SINCE LAST YEAR.

THE GLACIER'S COMING!!
THE GLACIER'S COMING!!
9·1

two idiots trapped in a
revolving door

HI THERE! I AM AN APTERYX, A BIRDLESS HAIR WITH WINGY FEA...UH......

SOB
THERE THERE...
9·3

...WE CAN ALWAYS USE IT AS AN OUT-TAKE.

DO YOU HAVE THE NATIONAL ANTHEM BY ROBERT GOULET?
PETER'S MUSIC STORE

YES.
WHICH VERSION WOULD YOU LIKE,

OVER OR UNDER THE COUNTER?
PETER'S MUSIC STORE

9·5

THAT'S WHERE THE WHOLE GROUP PLAYS THE SAME SONG AT ONCE

PETER'S MUSIC STORE

hart

I'D LIKE THE LATEST RELEASE BY "GLADYS KNIGHT AND THE PIPS."
THE $4.99 OR $6.95 VERSION?
PETER'S MUSIC STORE

WHAT'S THE DIFFERENCE?

THE 4.99 ONLY FEATURES ONE PIP.
PETER'S MUSIC STORE
9.7
hart

DO YOU SELL SHEET MUSIC?
WE PRIDE OURSELVES ON HAVING EVERY SONG THAT'S EVER BEEN WRITTEN.
PETER'S MUSIC STORE

GOOD, I'D LIKE THE TAMBOURINE CHART TO THE 1812 OVERTURE.

.... SOLD THE LAST ONE THIS MORNING.
PETER'S MUSIC STORE

9·8

Hart

WHAT'S THE LATEST SINGLE BY THE 'ALUMINUM FROG'?
PETER'S MUSIC STORE

WHY DON'T YOU STICK A PICKLE IN YOUR EAR AND GET OFF MY BACK!
9.9

...THEN ON THE FLIP-SIDE, THERE'S....
PETER'S MUSIC STORE

I'D LIKE "BE MY LOVE" BY MARIO LANZA.
WITH OR WITHOUT THE INSURANCE RIDER?
PETER'S MUSIC STORE

INSURANCE?

....FOR YOUR PICTURE WINDOWS.
PETER'S MUSIC STORE
9·10

SON·OF·A·GUN,
..A LADYBUG!
hart

ZOT

9.12

...WAS YOUR MOTHER DRIVING A VOLKSWAGEN?

I'D LIKE TWO ACE SPINNERS, A RED DEUCE PLUG, AND A SHAKESPEARE JOKER.
CLUMSY'S BAIT SHOP

9·13

...AND KEEP YOUR HANDS ABOVE THE TABLE.
CLUMSY'S BAIT SHOP

IN THE INTEREST OF ECOLOGY, I THINK I'LL DISCONTINUE THE WHEEL.

WHAT IN THE WORLD FOR?

9.14

IT'S AN EARTH GUZZLER.

PETER'S
BANK

9·16

I WAS JUST ABOUT TO MAKE A WITHDRAWAL !
CLOSED
GONE FISHING

.....AND I JUST BEAT YOU TO IT.
CLOSED
GONE FISHING

DO YOU REALIZE THAT TO KISS ONE MAN IS TO SET OUR CAUSE BACK 3 YEARS?

9.17

I DIDN'T KNOW THAT.

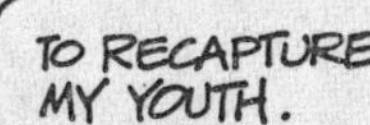

WHERE ARE YOU GOING?
TO RECAPTURE MY YOUTH.

LAST
CHANC
9·19

E

WHAT'S YOUR KINKIEST MAGAZINE?
MAGAZINES
9.20

"CARTOON TURN-ONS"

..PINOCCHIO...
MAGAZINES

THOR!...
9·24

WHAT HAPPENED?

FACE LIFT.
hart

BEHOLD.... THE GREATEST INVENTION SINCE THE WHEEL...
10·1

WHAT'S THAT ?

THE SPARE.

WHO WAS THE EXECUTIVE PRODUCER FOR "THE GREATEST STORY EVER WRITTEN"?
TRIVIA TEST

ZOT

NO COACHING FROM THE AUDIENCE, PLEASE!
TRIVIA TEST

WHO HOLDS THE RECORD FOR THE WORLD'S LONGEST APPLE PEEL?
TRIVIA TEST
10-4

I GIVE UP. ...WHO?

GYPSY ROSE McINTOSH.
TRIVIA TEST

WHO IS RESPONSIBLE FOR BUILDING THE LONGEST UNDER-WATER TUNNEL ?
TRIVIA TEST

THE LINCOLN FERRET.
TRIVIA TEST

10·7

WAS THE PLUMB-BOB INVENTED BEFORE OR AFTER THE CONSTRUCTION OF THE LEANING TOWER OF PISA ?
TRIVIA TEST

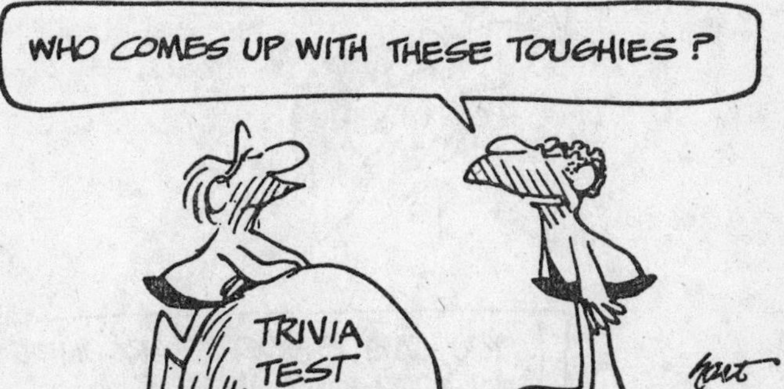
WHO COMES UP WITH THESE TOUGHIES ?
TRIVIA TEST

10·8

DO YOU REALLY NEED TO WEAR GLASSES, CLUMSY ?
LET ME PUT IT THIS WAY....
10·10

..WHAT YOUR WOODEN LEG IS TO YOU,.... MY GLASSES ARE TO ME.

YOU CARRY BOOZE AROUND IN YOUR GLASSES ?
hart.

SNIFF
SNIFF

10.11

HELP YOURSELF, GROG.
MUNCH
MUNCH
CRUNCH
CRACKLE
SLURP
GULP
GULP

YOU COULD HAVE LEFT THE @#★★!! FIRE!
BURP

...RICKY-TICKY-TEE ...
ZIPPY-DIPPY-DIPPY-DOO....
10-13

HEY! THAT'S CATCHY. WHERE DID YOU LEARN THAT?

I USED TO BE BOP-VOCALIST WITH GUY LOMBARDO.

GO AHEAD, RUN OFF WITH "PROVOCATIVE SHIRLEY."

...JUST DON'T EXPECT ME TO BE HERE WHEN THE FLING IS OVER!
10·14
"PROVOCATIVE SHIRLEY" ONLY BOOKS FLINGS?

OK...TELL ME MY FORTUNE.
FORTUNES TOLD 5 CLAMS

10.15

..FOUR THOUSAND, FIFTY-SIX DOLLARS AND 63 CENTS.

..LESS 5 CLAMS....
FORTUNES TOLD 5 CLAMS

OH, OH, ...MY NOSE ITCHES.

THAT MEANS I'M GOING TO KISS A FOOL.
10·17

...$E=MC^2$.... THE SQUARE OF THE HYPOTENUSE IS EQUAL TO...UH...

...I'VE BEEN HERE BEFORE.

YOU'RE ONE OF THOSE WEIRDOS THAT BELIEVE IN REINCARNATION, RIGHT ?
NOT REALLY.
10-18

...YESTERDAY I WAS HERE.
hart

I NEED LOVE...

...FROM SOMEBODY!
...ANYBODY!....
10·19

WHAM
WHAM
WHAM
WHAM
WHAM

15 mi. TO HOTEL
14 mi. TO HOTEL
10·20
...THEY'RE CARRYING THE #@*#!! THIRTEEN SYNDROME A BIT TOO FAR!
12 mi. TO HOTEL

HOW DO YOU TELL THE AGE OF A TREE?
BY THE RINGS.

RING
10·21

HAPPY BIRTHDAY.

WHAT DOES "INC." MEAN?
BEATS THE HECK OUT OF ME. WHO WANTS TO KNOW?
RESEARCH INC.
10·22

I WANT TO KNOW!

THEN LOOK IT UP.
RESEARCH INC.

WANNA SMELL MY FLOWER?
HA! THAT'S THE OLDEST TRICK IN THE BOOK.
10·24

TRICK?
SORRY

SNIF

WE'RE GOING TO HAVE THE WORST WINTER IN HISTORY!
WHO SAYS SO?

I JUST SAW A WOOLLY WORM!
EVERY YEAR WE SEE WOOLLY WORMS!
10·25

.....WITH SKI MASKS?

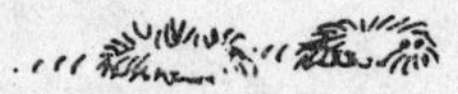
BOY, WE'RE IN FOR A ROUGH WINTER, ... LOOK AT THE SIZE OF THOSE WOOLLY WORMS!
10·26

WE'RE IN FOR A TOUGH WINTER, ACE, LOOK AT THE SIZE OF THOSE BUNIONS!

WHAT DO YOU THINK I'D LOOK LIKE IN A DORTHY HAMILL HAIRCUT ?

10·27

BOBBY ORR IN DRAG.

I'M SIGNING UP EVERYONE FOR THE HALLOWEEN PARTY.
YOU CAN PUT ME DOWN.
10·29

IS GROG COMING WITH YOU THIS YEAR?
NO

GOOD,... WE CAN SCRATCH THE "PUMPKIN BOBBING CONTEST"

KNOCK
KNOCK

TRICK OR TREAT.
10-31

ONLY A FOOL WOULD GO FOR THE TREAT.

...SORRY I MISSED THE HALLOWEEN PARTY.

11·1

WHO WON THE PRIZE FOR THE MOST FRIGHTENING COSTUME ?
THE FAT BROAD.

WHAT DID SHE COME AS?

LADY GODIVA.

DANGER
TURN
BACK

11·2

LONGITUDE 30 DEGREES,
LATITUDE 42 DEGREES...

ZOT
11·3

UNCLE BENEDICT!
...SAVE US!

WOW,...
LOOK AT
THAT!

WHAT IS
IT, ACE?
PUNT
11·4

"I DON'T KNOW, BUT IT
PULLS A LOT OF G's"

OH,OH,..A TELEGRAM. BAD NEWS.
THEN AGAIN, IT MIGHT BE GOOD NEWS.
WHAT THE HECK...
RIP
CONGRATULATIONS, YOU HAVE WON A SPOT IN THE "CELEBRITY TENNIS DOUBLES TOURNAMENT." YOUR PARTNER IS HOWARD COSELL.
IT'S BOTH.

TELL ME YOU LOVE ME OR I'LL BASH YOUR BRAINS OUT.

I LOVE YOU.

11.9

SWEAR ON YOUR GRANDMOTHER'S GRAVE!
I SWEAR ON MY GRANDMOTHER'S GRAVE.

TELEGRAM FROM YOUR GRANDMOTHER.
..OH NO.....

SNAIL·O·GRAM

HEY, LOOK AT THIS.
WHAT IS IT?

11·10

MY BIRTH ANNOUNCEMENT.

COLLECT TELEGRAM FROM YOUR MOTHER·IN·LAW.

I'M NOT PAYING ANY MONEY FOR BAD NEWS. RETURN IT TO THE SENDER.
I CAN'T DO THAT,...SHE KICKED OFF YESTERDAY.
11·11

HOW MUCH IS IT?

TELEGRAM FROM CLUMSY CARP.
YOU OPENED MY TELEGRAM!
11·12

I DID NOT!
THEN HOW CAN YOU TELL IT'S FROM CLUMSY CARP?

AAAARRGGHHH

...HELLO..
WHAT'S THIS?

OH.
IT'S ONLY ME.
11-14

Z

IT'S ONLY ME?

EITHER I'M DREAMING OR THAT ROCK MADE A SENTENCE...

YOU WERE JUST DREAMING
THANK HEAVENS
11-15

IT DID IT AGAIN!
hart

I DON'T SUPPOSE YOU HAVE A NAME...

CALL ME ROCKY
THAT'S PRETTY CORNY!
11·16

DON'T LAUGH I KNOW A STUMP NAMED WOODY

11·17

I'M GOING TO
WASH UP.
BE RIGHT
BACK.
YOU MOVE
TOO?
DARN
RIGHT
11-18
WILL YOU
SCRUB MY
BACK?
SURE.
WHERE IS IT?

PETER'S
PAWN
SHOP

PETER'S
PAWN
SHOP
HANG
IN
GUYS
11.19

RIGHT
ON
ROCKY

ARE YOU THE ONLY COMMUNICATING ROCK AROUND ?
NO, I HAVE HUNDREDS OF FRIENDS

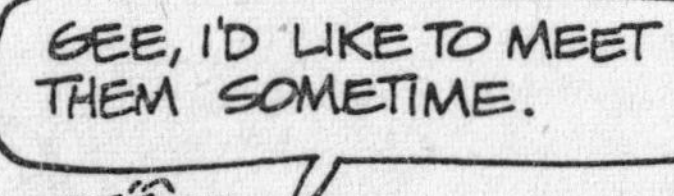
GEE, I'D LIKE TO MEET THEM SOMETIME.

WHY DON'T YOU COME WITH ME NEXT WEEKEND

11·21

WERE HOLDING AN AVALANCHE

THIS IS MY FRIEND ROCKY. SAY HI TO CLUMSY CARP, ROCKY.
HI

HEY THAT'S TERRIFIC! HOW DID IT DO THAT?

11 22

HE'S A ROCKTRILOQUIST

MERCY, MERCY, ...
WHERE CAN I HIDE?
OH...THANK
YOU!
GET THEE
BEHIND
ME
11·23

THAT'S THOR, THE RENOWNED INVENTOR OF THE WHEEL.

11·25

HE CHISELED A MASTERPIECE OUT OF A WORTHLESS ROCK.

SO THATS WHAT HAPPENED TO UNCLE ERNIE

WANNA GO FISHING?
TOO COLD

WANNA GO HUNTING?
TOO HOT.
11·28

WANNA NECK?

FISHING IT IS!

WHERE IN THE HECK DO YOU THINK YOU'RE GOING?

TO AN EXECUTIVE CONVENTION IN MINNEAPOLIS.
YOU'RE KIDDING! YOU'VE NEVER HAD A JOB IN YOUR LIFE!
11·29

IT DOESN'T MATTER!... I'M THE KEYNOTE SPEAKER.

DAD,...BEFORE I SHOW YOU MY REPORT CARD....
11·30

..LET ME REMIND YOU THAT EINSTEIN'S PARENTS CONSIDERED HIM A "DOLT" TILL HE PASSED PUBERTY.

...THAT'S NOT EVEN ON YOUR CURRICULUM, YOU DOLT!
hart

BEHOLD, THE WORLD'S LARGEST DIVINING ROD.

WHAT DO YOU EXPECT TO FIND WITH THAT?
JAMB
12·1

THE PACIFIC OCEAN!

WHAT'S WITH THE BIG SMILE?

I'M LOOKING AT THE BRIGHT SIDE OF LIFE TODAY.
ISN'T THAT HARD?

12·2

IF YOU DON'T MOVE ALONG, IT'S GOING TO BE IMPOSSIBLE.

WHATTA YA GOT HANGING OUTTA YOUR MOUTH THERE?

IT'S MY ULTIMATE SAFETY DEVICE: "THE AIR BAG." JUST BEFORE IMPACT, YOU BLOW IT UP AND IT CUSHIONS THE CRASH.
12-3

SHOULD BE A BIG SELLER ON WALL STREET.

ROCKY, I'D LIKE YOU TO MEET MY FRIEND CURLY.
12·5

...CURLY IS THE MASTER OF SARCASTIC WIT.

SAY SOMETHING SURLY

THAT'S QUITE A LISP YOU HAVE THERE

HI
12·6

HI

I CAN
DIG IT

THIS IS ONE OF MY DEAR FRIENDS, ROCKY,..SAY SOMETHING SWEET TO HER.

...ROCKY...

12·7

A TALKING ROCK. THE JOKE'S ON ME, RIGHT? ......REAL CUTE!
KONK

WHY DIDN'T YOU SAY SOMETHING?
WHO NEEDS ARMAGEDDON

DR.
PETER
↔
HEAD
SHRINKER
12·9

WHAT IN
THE WORLD
IS A HEAD
SHRINKER?

DR.
PETER
↔
HEAD
SHRINKER
DON'T ASK
ME, I'M JUST
THE COUCH

WHAT'S THAT?
THAT'S A PYRAMID OF SNOWBALLS.
SNOWTIME INC.

WHAT'S THAT?
THAT'S A BALL OF SNOW PYRAMIDS.
SNOWTIME INC.
12·14
A BALL OF SNOW PYRA....
GIVES THE PLACE A BALANCE.

GIVE IT UP, ACE, YOU HAVEN'T GOT A SNOWBALL'S CHANCE.
RECTANGULAR ICE CUBES CHEAP!

IGLOOS
12.15

...HELLO?...
IGLOOS

EEEYESSSS?
IGLOOS

WHAT CAN I GIVE A GUY WHO HAS NOTHING?
GIFT SUGGESTIONS
12·19

THE WRONG TELEPHONE NUMBER.
GIFT SUGGESTIONS

THE WIFE AND I DECIDED TO GIVE EACH OTHER NOTHING THIS YEAR.
12·20

WHAT KIND OF CHRISTMAS SPIRIT IS THAT?

WHO SAID ANYTHING ABOUT CHRISTMAS?
hart

WHAT'S THAT?
MISTLETOE.

HOW MANY LUCKY DEVILS HAVE YOU NAILED SO FAR?
JUST ONE. ..AND THAT WAS 12 HOURS AGO.
12·22

BEWARE OF THE MISTLETOE

WHAT DO YOU WANT FOR CHRISTMAS, MOM?

ALL MOMMY WANTS IS FOR YOU TO BE A GOOD BOY, PULL STRAIGHT A'S AND MAKE FIRST-STRING QUARTERBACK...
12·23

HOW MUCH ARE YOUR MINK-COATS?
GIFTS
hart

Z

GET LOST
YOU OLD
GEEZER!
Z

I'D LIKE TO EXCHANGE THIS CHESS SET, IT'S MISSING TWO PIECES!
EXCHANGES
12·26

ARE THEY THE CASTLES?
AS A MATTER OF FACT, YES!

YOU'RE THE THIRD GUY THIS WEEK THAT GOT ROOKED.
EXCHANGES

12·27

I WORE THE NIFTY NEW SHOES YOU GAVE ME FOR CHRISTMAS.

ID LIKE TO EXCHANGE THIS BOOK.
EXCHANGES

HMM...."1000 AND ONE WAYS TO LOSE UGLY FAT."
WHAT WOULD YOU LIKE TO EXCHANGE IT FOR?
12·28

2 MINUTES IN THE RING WITH WHOEVER SENT IT TO ME.
EXCHANGES

I HEAR THE FAT BROAD IS HAVING A KNOCK-DOWN, DRAG-OUT, NEW YEAR'S "BASH". ...DID YOU GET AN INVITATION?
NO.

12·30

NEITHER DID I!
THAT'S ODD.

WHAT'S ODD, IS: I GOT MINE SPECIAL DELIVERY.